Mending Fences

Mending Fences

A Guide for Rebuilding Your Relationships

NANCY WEYER

Foreword by David L. Allen

RESOURCE *Publications* · Eugene, Oregon

MENDING FENCES
A Guide for Rebuilding Your Relationships

Resource Publications
An Imprint of Wipf and Stock Publishers
199 W. 8th Ave., Suite 3
Eugene, OR 97401

www.wipfandstock.com

PAPERBACK ISBN: 978-1-6667-3366-2
HARDCOVER ISBN: 978-1-6667-2851-4
EBOOK ISBN: 978-1-6667-2852-1

01/28/22

This book was inspired by Jesus. It was he who was with me and who guided me through the experiences that produced this work, and it was by his Word that I learned the principles contained herein.

Thank you, Lord Jesus. I pray you are glorified.

Contents

Foreword

by David L. Allen

THE NUMBER ONE STRUGGLE in all our lives is relationships. Whether marriage, parenting, friendship, or work, relationships are really the bottom line for all of us. The relationships we do have sometimes become strained or even broken. What we need is a reliable guide to rebuilding relationships.

The book you have in your hand is just that. It is not a self-help book. Those are a dime a dozen, and many are not worth your dime or your time. *Mending Fences* is a substantive, simple, biblical, and practical book with keen insights into Scripture and human nature. Nancy Weyer understands both and deftly weaves the two together in a beautiful tapestry of spiritual and psychological help.

Reading this book will make you think the author has been reading your mail, if not your mind. Somehow, she has the uncanny ability to put her finger on just the right spot of need. Her bedside manner is calm and reassuring. With a clear, warm, and engaging writing style, Dr. Weyer puts you at ease so that you feel normal about your struggles and realize the suggestions she offers are an efficacious tonic for your soul. The reader is treated like a friend not a client.

Sometimes when books purport to integrate biblical truth with psychological insight, the result is a distortion of one or the other, or both. This book is thoroughly biblical and grounds all psychology in Scripture. We sometimes forget that the Bible itself, rather than being an antiquated book, is chock full of psychological truth and insight. With a perfect blend of Scripture and good psychology, Dr. Weyer writes a prescription that works.

The format of the book is easy to follow and implement. Each chapter contains three elements: content, action, and journal. The author gives us something to learn, something to practice, and something to journal. The length of each section is not overwhelming. Even those, like me, who are not much into journaling, will find this section succinct in writing down your own thoughts. The book is designed to be read and digested over a period of ten weeks.

Encouragement is what so many of us need in this topsy-turvy world, and *Mending Fences* does not disappoint. This is not a book that attempts to change the other person to your satisfaction; it is a book that attempts to help you change yourself. In marriage, the fundamental of all relationships, the issue is not finding the right person, or changing your spouse, but rather it is being the right person. Think of the principles in this book as tools to help you repair relationships. The repair process begins with you.

Change comes when we know something and then do something. The action-oriented assignments in this book follow the biblical insights taught. This allows the reader to put into practice James 1:22: "*Be doers of the word and not hearers only, deceiving yourselves*" (CSB). James is reminding us that we must do more than audit Scripture; we must enroll in the class! In academia, auditors enjoy the class lectures, but are not required to do any of the class assignments. But at the end of the semester, when grades are given, auditors earn no credit for the class either. This book will help you do more than be an auditor of Scripture. It will help you enroll in the class . . . and get credit for your work.

As Dr. Weyer has said: "At a time in our nation when chaos reigns and relationships are strained, many believers are looking for answers in Christian self-help books based in secular humanism. This book departs from others because it offers answers that can bring about lasting change using only Scriptural principles. Pastors, counselors, and individuals who use this book will not have to wonder if the solutions offered are in line with Scripture because Scripture, not psychology, is its foundation."

If you approach this book in the right spirit, with a humble heart to learn and a commitment to follow the biblical principles Dr. Weyer lays out for you, you will be well on your way to relationship repair. You will learn the master secret of moving from "Lord, change him or her" to "Lord, change me!"

Preface

As someone who studied psychology all my adult life, I thought I had gained such a vast assortment of tools for working with troubled relationships that I could help anyone. My bachelor's degree is in psychology, my master's degree is in marital and family therapy, and my doctorate is in professional counseling. Yet even with all this formal education, I still felt my knowledge base was somehow incomplete. I knew the Bible offered wisdom about how to have healthy relationships, but I was unable to piece its wisdom together into a comprehensive and manageable whole.

Then, beginning in 2011 and continuing through 2017, the Lord began to show me specifically what his Word has to say about relationships. I had studied the Bible for twenty-five years prior to that time, but during those six years the focus for my daily quiet time with him was almost exclusively on the application of his Word to relationships. Once I began to apply these principles to my own challenging relationship issues, I saw the supernatural work of the Lord in areas where psychological tools had made no difference. This book is the product of those years of instruction.

Acknowledgments

I AM GRATEFUL TO Wipf and Stock for publishing this book. As a first-time author I realize you are taking a risk on the marketability of this work, and I appreciate the opportunity immensely. I also appreciate the help of my editor at Wipf and Stock, Matthew Wimer. Matt, thank you for patiently answering the many questions I asked. You were long-suffering with me, and I appreciate your assistance and kindness.

Because this book's subject matter required accurate biblical interpretation with correct application, I needed the aid of subject matter experts to ensure the work was theologically sound. The Lord very graciously provided me access to several outstanding Bible authorities who did that and much more.

First among those Bible scholars is the pastor of Lake Shore Baptist Church and my friend of many years Homer Walkup. Pastor Homer spent countless hours discipling me for ten years about how to apply biblical principles to life. Ultimately, that instruction also impacted how I wrote this book. Pastor Homer, thank you for selflessly sharing your time and your vast wisdom with me. You have shaped my thinking and my life. Second, it is beyond my comprehension how Dr. David Allen (the Director of the Southwestern Center for Expository Preaching at Southwestern Baptist Theological Seminary) took the time to even read my manuscript. Not only did he read it without ever having met me, but he also ushered me into the presence of several of his publishers, and then even wrote the foreword to this book. Thank you, Dr. Allen, for spending so much of your precious time on this book. I do not think I could have received a higher form of praise than your willingness to help me get it published. A fourth significant influence on my belief that this work was theologically solid was the approval of the senior pastor of Denton Bible Church, Tommy Nelson. Pastor Nelson not only read my manuscript and encouraged me to have it published, but he also gave me a foot in the door to one of his publishers. As I waited and wondered if the book would ever be published, he told me to write another book after this one was done because he said, "A writer's got to write!" Pastor Nelson, you cannot imagine how many times those words have reverberated in my head and how encouraging that was coming from you. Thank you so much for your assistance and support. Finally, another eminent Bible scholar whom I owe a debt of gratitude is Dr. Daniel Akin. I shake my head in wonderment as to how God connected me, a person of no standing, with a world-renowned scholar such as the President of Southeastern Baptist Theological Seminary! Dr. Akin, having your approval on this work assured me I could pursue publication with confidence. Thank you so very much.

I cannot envision what it would have been like to write this book without the help of my family and my friends. First, I want to thank my husband who allowed me to steal away for days on end to write this book at the beach: the place where inspiration abounds for me. Thank you, Doug, for giving me the enormous amount of time I needed to pray and think and write the material in this book. Secondly, I want to thank my mother, stepfather, son, daughter-in-law, daughter, son-in-law, sister, brother-in-law, and my friends who all contributed to the book's completion by standing by me as I walked the faith journey that was the source material for this book. I know it was often painful to watch me struggle but, as you can see, Jesus brought me victoriously through to the end. Thank you for your love, encouragement, and for your many prayers.

Acknowledgments

I also want to thank my family, friends, and colleagues who read and lovingly critiqued my manuscripts. Thank you for your love, your words of encouragement, and your corrections. Thank you also for your willingness to share so personally of yourselves to help me understand what was good and what needed improvement in the original drafts of this material.

Finally, I want to thank my son Jonathan Cochran for his help in writing "The Plan of Salvation" at the end of this book. Jonathan, your understanding of Scripture is deep and wide, and I am amazed at all God has revealed to you about his Word. Thank you for patiently sharing your knowledge with me.

Introduction

AN IMPORTANT DISTINCTION SHOULD be made between using a psychological self-help book and the approach taken in this book employing biblical wisdom. Most psychological theories on relationship counseling seek to alter peoples' interactional patterns where the objective is to have both parties in the relationship change. By contrast, the concepts based upon Scripture used in this book are aimed at changing the reader. Therefore, if you are looking for a book to "fix" the person with whom you have a challenging relationship, this is probably not the right resource for you. In this book, you will not be using strategies or techniques designed to change the other person, they are designed to change you. As you read this book and do the activities, it is certainly possible God will work on the other person while he is working on you. However, your focus should not be on what he or she is doing, instead it should be on your own thoughts, feelings, and actions.

Any relationship you would like to improve can benefit from the tools provided in this book: spouse, parent, son, daughter, friend, sibling, co-worker, *et cetera*. As you prepare to do this study, it is important to remember this: damaged relationships do not become damaged in a day, a month, or even in a year—therefore, repairing them takes time. Relationships are complex and multifaceted and in order to address their many angles, a wealth of information over a significant period of time is needed.

This book covers a span of ten weeks and at the end of the ten weeks I encourage you to go back to the beginning and start again. In fact, you can read and do the activities in this book multiple times. While it may seem like a big commitment to spend so many weeks reading and doing the suggested activities in this book, it is less than one year you are investing in a change process that could heal a relationship that has caused you a tremendous amount of pain and stress. My question to you is, would it be worth an investment of ten weeks, twenty weeks, or more to give you tools offering peace of mind with a relationship that has troubled you for years?

HOW TO USE THIS BOOK

Every Monday, Wednesday, and Friday you will have a new concept presented which you will work on for two days. I recommend you set aside at least fifteen minutes every morning for this study and do only one lesson at a time. Before you begin each study time, ask God for his wisdom, power, and strength regarding the relationship(s) with which you are struggling.

At the beginning of each section, you will find this symbol ▣ next to Scripture with a description about how to apply the passage(s) to your relationship. Next, you will come to the Action section where you will find this symbol 🏃 with instructions for practical application of the Scripture. At the end of each day, you will return to the book to the Journal section where you will see this symbol ✏. You should plan to spend about fifteen minutes thinking and writing about how the Scripture and the Action assignment in that section impacted you and/or your troubled relationship(s). You can choose to be as detailed or as vague as you want in the journal section (you may even want to get a notebook so you can have extra space to write). The point of having a place to write is to help you remember how you and/or your relationship were impacted by the Scriptures and/or the assignments (I probably don't need to tell you how forgetful we humans can be!). Finally, to provide further help with memorizing the concepts, every other Friday you will find this symbol ⮌ where the principles from the previous five lessons are reviewed. You will spend the review lesson recalling and practicing what you learned in the preceding lessons. You will also notice on the review day a reminder to be praying daily since the source for your strength and success in your relationship(s) is from the Lord.

Author's note: I have written this book using the pronoun "he," "him," and "his" throughout when referring to the person or people with whom you are in a difficult relationship, understanding it may be a female. I did this for simplicity's sake so the reading would not be cumbersome.

Monday

📖 *This is my command: Love each other. (John 15:17)*

WHEN WE TALK ABOUT love in the English language, our terminology is imprecise. I might say "I love spaghetti" and then use the same word when I say "I love my husband." I assume the people who hear me know my feelings for spaghetti are quite different from those I have for my husband, but the word "love" itself does not convey that difference in meaning. Fortunately, the vocabulary of the Greek language used in the New Testament is more precise. When we learn the Greek word for love, we can gain insight into this passage's meaning so we can accurately apply it in our relationships.

In John 15:17 when Jesus said, *"This is my command: Love each other,"* he used the term *agape (agapaō)* which means to have good-will toward another; to consider the welfare of another; to act upon another's welfare independent of our feelings.[1] Therefore, when Jesus said, "This is my command: Love each other," he was not asking for an emotional response. He was commanding us to be intentionally thinking about and acting in the best interests of others.

Let me give you some other verses where the term agape is used to provide further clarification about this very important

1. Blue Letter Bible, "*agapaō.*"

word. In Ephesians 5:1–2, the apostle Paul wrote, "*Follow God's example, therefore, as dearly loved children and walk in the way of love, just as Christ loved us and gave himself up for us as a fragrant offering and sacrifice to God.*" In this verse, Paul tells us to pattern the way we relate to others as God relates to us. He reminds us that Christ showed his love to us by sacrificing his life, and he tells us we are to do the same for each other. In John 13:34 Jesus said, "*A new command I give you: Love one another. As I have loved you, so you must love one another.*" Here Jesus compels us once again to love others in the same manner he loved us.

So, let me ask you, what comes to mind when you think about the ways Jesus loves you? Do you think about how Jesus feels for you, or do you think about the ways he has demonstrated his love for you? To put this in terms of your earthly relationships, ask yourself these questions. How would I know if someone loved me? Would it be enough if someone merely tells me he feels love for me, or would I need concrete evidence of that love to be certain? I am sure at some point you would need actual proof to know definitively if a person truly loved you. The same is true in all these passages of Scripture: the focus of love is about action not feeling. Agape acts in the best interests of people every day and on every occasion, regardless of feeling. Now of course, no one is perfect and there will be times when you will not act in a loving way. However, the truth is the kind of love God requires of us is the kind we act upon intentionally and consistently with all the people in our lives.

🏃 ACTION

In this assignment, you will be focusing on acting in ways to demonstrate your love toward the person with whom you have a challenging relationship. To begin, think about the ways Jesus has shown his love for you. Reflect on the fact Christ showed his love by dying for you while you were still in sin, not because you were good and had earned his love and his sacrifice: "*But God demonstrates his own love for us in this: While we were still sinners, Christ died for us*" (Rom 5:8); "*But because of his great love for us, God, who is rich in mercy, made us alive with Christ even when we were dead in transgressions—it is by grace you have been saved"* (Eph 2:4–5). When we remember God loved us even while we were dead in our sins, it can motivate us to love the people we find difficult to get along with just the way they are. Additionally, remembering God's loving acts toward us can stir gratitude in our hearts, and gratitude has a wonderful way of softening us to act with love toward others.

The next step involves putting love into action. Start thinking about ways to act lovingly toward the other person today. Think about things he likes or needs, make a list of those things, and then do them. Be sure you think about what the other person likes or needs and not what you like or want for him.

✒ **JOURNAL**

_____

_____

_____

_____

_____

_____

Wednesday

You were taught, with regard to your former way of life, to put off your old self, which is being corrupted by its deceitful desires; to be made new in the attitude of your minds; and to put on the new self, created to be like God in true righteousness and holiness. Therefore, each of you must put off falsehood and speak truthfully to your neighbor, for we are all members of one body. In your anger do not sin: do not let the sun go down while you are still angry, and do not give the devil a foothold. Anyone who has been stealing must steal no longer, but must work, doing something useful with their own hands, that they may have something to share with those in need. Do not let any unwholesome talk come out of your mouths, but only what is helpful for building others up according to their needs, that it may benefit those who listen. (Eph 4:22–25, 29)

Do not lie to each other, since you have taken off your old self with its practices and have put on the new self, which is being renewed in knowledge in the image of its Creator. Here there is no Gentile or Jew, circumcised or uncircumcised, barbarian, Scythian, slave or free, but Christ is all, and is in all. Therefore, as God's chosen people, holy and dearly loved, clothe yourselves with compassion, kindness, humility, gentleness, and patience. (Col 3:9–12)

THE VERSES IN EPHESIANS 4 and Colossians 3 describe "putting off" and "putting on" certain types of behaviors. For example, we are told to put off falsehood and instead to speak the truth. Additionally, we are instructed to clothe ourselves with compassion, kindness, humility, gentleness, and patience. When we try to change the way we speak or act, an important principle to keep in mind is this: generally speaking, we cannot simply stop doing one behavior without replacing that behavior with something else. The reason for this is if you stop engaging in a behavior you have done for a while without doing something different in its place, you will eventually fall back into your old ways. Let me give you an example.

Imagine two sisters who I will call Lisa and Abigail. When the two sisters get together, they spend a great deal of time gossiping about the members of their family. Lisa eventually becomes a Christian and is convicted about her sinful words with her sister, so she decides to put an end to the gossip. The first time she gets together with Abigail, Lisa can resist the temptation to join in with her when she starts talking negatively about their family. However, the next time they are together, even though Lisa tries not to talk about their family in a negative way, when Abigail starts gossiping, she eventually gives in. She convinces herself their conversation is necessary to convey "vital" information to each other. Later that day, Lisa is convicted again by her sin and does not know how she will ever stop doing what they have done for so many years. She has told her sister she does not want to gossip anymore, but Abigail does not understand why Lisa wants to stop talking about others the way they always have.

Now picture the same situation with Lisa and Abigail, but this time Lisa pays attention to the specific instructions given in the preceding verses. She takes note of the fact they tell her to take off one behavior and put on something else in its place, so Lisa makes a plan to stop gossiping and instead to change the subject when Abigail starts talking about the family. She pays close attention to the part of the verse in Ephesians 4:29 which states, "*Do not let any unwholesome talk come out of your mouths, but only what is helpful for building others up according to their needs, that it may benefit those who listen."* Lisa thinks of some specific things she can talk about that will be helpful to her sister the next time they are together. She then pictures in her mind the future conversation with Abigail so she is ready when they meet again. She imagines herself speaking the words she has planned, how she will feel when she is saying them, and how she will be at peace about her conversation afterward.

The next time they meet, Lisa is able to resist the urge to gossip even though Abigail still tries to engage her in that way. She remembers the things she planned to talk about and finds it is helpful to have something to fill the void where she used to gossip. In the future, every time Lisa gets ready to see her sister, she prepares in the same way and can then avoid gossiping.

The two examples of the sisters illustrate how you can change entrenched behavioral patterns by replacing old behaviors with new ones. One idea that also may be helpful is using mental rehearsal, just like Lisa did in the second example. Visualizing an activity before you engage in it can give you a greater chance of success than if you had not mentally rehearsed it beforehand. In fact, athletes often credit their success in part to their repetitious mental rehearsal (e.g., basketball players imagine making perfect free throws and baseball players imagine hitting the ball over the fence). Mental rehearsal is helpful for almost anything you want to accomplish from sports to public speaking, and today you will be applying it to your relationship(s).

ACTION

Think about some of the actions, thoughts, and words currently damaging your relationship. Pray and ask God to help you let go of these destructive patterns. Remember also that you are engaged in a spiritual battle and the only way you can be successful is through the power of the Holy Spirit: *"Finally, be strong in the Lord and in his mighty power. Put on the full armor of God, so that you can take your stand against the devil's schemes. For our struggle is not against flesh and blood, but against the rulers, against the authorities, against the powers of this dark world and against the spiritual forces of evil in the heavenly realms"* (Eph 6:10–12). Then, in place of the damaging actions, thoughts, and words, imagine yourself putting on some of the adjectives described in Ephesians 4 and Colossians 3. For example, if you find yourself speaking untruthfully in your relationship, imagine speaking the truth to him. If you tend to be harsh, imagine yourself speaking gentle words with humility. If you are holding unforgiveness in your heart toward him, imagine placing the wrongs he has done to you into God's hands.

When you are envisioning yourself with the other person, picture clearly in your mind how you will take off one type of unpleasant or destructive behavior and then will put on behavior that is Christlike, just as if you were taking off one set of clothes and putting on a new set. Imagine the words you will be saying to the other person, your body posture when you are with him, and your facial expressions. In this way, you are mentally rehearsing the specific details of how you want to be when you are together. The next time you are with him, put these behaviors and words into action.

✎ JOURNAL

Friday

Love is patient, love is kind. It does not envy, it does not boast, it is not proud. It does not dishonor others, it is not self-seeking, it is not easily angered, it keeps no record of wrongs. Love does not delight in evil but rejoices with the truth. It always protects, always trusts, always hopes, always perseveres. (1 Cor 13:4–7)

WHEN I WAS GROWING up, there were many songs on the radio that impacted my life without me even knowing it at the time. As is the case now, back in the 1970s many of the songs about relationships had inaccurate messages about the true meaning of love. For example, many of the songs I listened to suggested love was primarily about romance. They celebrated moonlit nights, candlelit dinners, walks on the beach, and other idealized moments. Their messages were not about maintaining commitment when the good times and feelings fade. Almost all the songs focused on emotions, personal gain, and selfish pleasures.

Movies and television shows were no less impactful on my life back then, as they depicted shallow, one-dimensional views of love. Romantic scenes were often the focus for marriages, and frequently friendships and other familial relationships were based on what people could selfishly get from others. Some storylines conveyed the idea that if people were difficult or did not satisfy one's needs and desires, they should be discarded. If people were deemed as needy or inconvenient, they were left behind in pursuit of other more "fulfilling" relationships.

Unfortunately, some of those ideas from songs and movies impacted me when I was an adolescent trying to understand the concept of love and it ended up having a negative impact on my view of love. It took me many years to learn love is primarily not about emotions or selfish gains at all, but instead is a set of actions and thoughts we must purposefully practice.

𝔁 ACTION

Today's Action involves replacing some of your negative words and actions toward the person with whom you have a difficult relationship with some of the descriptions of love given in 1 Corinthians 13:4–7. Regardless of how you are feeling about him, this assignment is about acting in loving ways without considering what you will get in return.

Here are a couple of examples of how you might do this. If you tend to be irritable with him, make it a goal to be patient and speak only kind words to him. If you tend to interrupt him when he is speaking, be careful to let him finish what he is saying before you speak. Reflect on the times God has demonstrated true love (i.e., agape) to you when you did not deserve it and pass it on. Choose two of the attributes of love described in 1 Corinthians 13:4–7 and find ways to express them.

✎ JOURNAL

_____

_____

_____

_____

_____

_____

Week 2

Monday

📖 *Lift up your eyes and look to the heavens: Who created all these? He who brings out the starry host one by one and calls forth each of them by name. Because of his great power and mighty strength, not one of them is missing. Why do you complain, Jacob? Why do you say, Israel, "My way is hidden from the LORD; my cause is disregarded by my God?" Do you not know? Have you not heard? The LORD is the everlasting God, the Creator of the ends of the earth. He will not grow tired or weary, and his understanding no one can fathom. He gives strength to the weary and increases the power of the weak. Even youths grow tired and weary, and young men stumble and fall; but those who hope in the LORD will renew their strength. They will soar on wings like eagles; they will run and not grow weary; they will walk and not be faint.* (Isa 40:26–31)

WHEN I WAS WORKING on my PhD, I spent many long days and nights tending to my family, my studies, and my job, and I simply did not have the ability to do everything well in my own strength. In my quiet times with the Lord, he regularly pointed me toward verses about his power and his strength and his willingness to share those attributes with me. Verses like those above in Isaiah assured me no detail of my life was outside of his protection and provision.

One way the Lord helped me remember his power was by calling my attention to the vast universe he created. There were many nights when I would stand outside and look up at the stars, reminding and encouraging myself that since God created and even took the time to name each one of them, he could certainly help me graduate, counsel others, raise the children he had given me, and give me his peace in the process.

Today's verses are some of my favorites when it comes to remembering who God is and all he can do on our behalf. Instead of allowing our focus to remain fixed on things of this world that concern us, we can redirect our attention to the heavens as a reminder of God's power and his desire to help us with every aspect of our lives.

In Isaiah 40:29–31 from today's verses, the Lord tells us he will give strength to those who "hope in" (i.e., look expectantly to)[1] him. Not only will God strengthen us, the word-picture painted here is God will cause us to "soar on wings like eagles," to "run and not grow weary," and to "walk and not be faint." In other words, God will not just help those who hope in him to muddle through or just get by: he will make them *walk, run,* and even *soar!* When we remember God made the heavens and the earth, we can rest assured he has the power to fulfill what he promises.

✷ ACTION

Go outside tonight and look at the stars. If you live in an area where you cannot see the stars or if the weather will not permit, look on the internet for information regarding the stars in our universe. As you reflect on what we know about them, consider the following from Isaiah 40:26 above:

- God creates each and every star.
- He leads them out (they are under his command).
- He names each one of them.

1. Barker, *NIV Study Bible,* 1073.

- His power sustains them all.

The next time you are troubled by your relationship, remember this evening spent under the stars and the power available to you from the One who creates them all. As you put your hope in him, his strength and power will supernaturally replace your weakness.

✎ JOURNAL

_____

_____

_____

_____

_____

_____

Wednesday

📖 *Be joyful in hope, patient in affliction, faithful in prayer. (Rom 12:12)*

LIFE CAN FEEL LIKE the ocean's waves. At times, you are riding high with the thrill of joyful experiences washing into your life, at other times you are flooded with bad news sending you crashing to the shore. When difficult times come, our troubled relationships can take an even heavier toll on us because they can drain our already depleted energy. Our natural emotional response to crises or difficult situations might be anger, fear, or desperation. These negative emotions can give way to destructive reactions such as arguing, complaining, and demanding, all of which intensify our distress. The good news is we do not need to let our natural reactions run our lives when difficult times arise.

Today's verse from Romans 12:12 gives us a great example of what to do when faced with trying circumstances: be joyful in hope, patient in affliction, and faithful in prayer. Wow! Did you notice those commands? *"Be joyful in hope, patient in affliction and faithful in prayer."* I don't know about you, but by my natural response to trials does not tend to be any of those. How do you tend to respond to a crisis? Do you remember God is in control of all situations which gives you a sense of joyful hope, or do you crumble in fear and anxiety worrying about what tomorrow might bring? If a difficult situation has been in your life for a while, are you patiently enduring it, or have you become angry, disgruntled, or bitter? Are you praying faithfully about your relationship, or have you given up and become apathetic about it?

✦ ACTION

Write Romans 12:12 on a sticky note and put it in a place where you will see it multiple times every day. Each time you come across it, do not just quickly glance over it. Instead, take time to reflect on the words. Examine your thoughts as you read it and make the necessary changes to line up your thinking with the commands given. Take note of how your thoughts and feelings change after applying these scriptural instructions and write the transformations below.

✏ JOURNAL

_____

_____

_____

_____

_____

_____

Friday

↩ **REVIEW**

- Look for ways to act lovingly toward him by meeting some of his wants or needs.
- Visualize yourself putting off any comments or conversations that are not uplifting and putting on uplifting and encouraging statements.
- Reflect on the attributes of love you expressed.
- Remember your evening under the stars and the majesty and power of God.
- Remember to be joyful in hope, patient in affliction, and faithful in prayer.
- Are you praying daily for your relationship?

✎ JOURNAL

_____

_____

_____

_____

_____

_____

Monday

A person's wisdom yield's patience; it is to one's glory to overlook
an offense. (Prov 19:11)

WHEN YOU ARE IN a challenging relationship, it seems almost anything the other person says or does can rub you the wrong way. For
instance, he might spend twenty minutes telling you about his day
and then never get around to asking you how your day was, causing you to think how this is a perfect example of his selfishness.
Or he may forget to call you as promised, and you ruminate on
how this reflects his irresponsible character. These things would
probably be insignificant if done by anyone else. However, when
the person with whom you are already struggling does them, they
become like stones heaped on a pile of an ever-growing mountain,
and that mountain is always present in your mind. You then may
feel compelled to let him know how he has wronged you, which
creates even greater tension.

But what would happen if instead of reacting to the offenses,
you chose to overlook them? You might be thinking if you do, he
will continue to offend you and it will only make the relationship
worse. Perhaps you are thinking it is important to communicate
how he offends you so he can change his behavior. While it is
true communication is important, let's compare how we typically

respond when we are offended in a good relationship to how we respond in a challenging one.

In a relationship free from constant disagreements and turmoil, when the person does something bothersome or hurtful to us, we quickly dismiss the offense and move on. We immediately think it is no big deal, and we can even bring ourselves to think about the positive qualities that person possesses. We do not hold onto the offense, nor do we give it a great deal of thought. Furthermore, we generally do not consider how a minor incident negatively reflects the other person's character. Then, because we have not held onto the offense, we do not focus on it the next time we are together.

Unfortunately, this is not the case in a difficult relationship where we typically add each new minor offense to the pile and examine it in detail. We mull it over in our minds for hours or even days, causing our irritations to grow and the heavy burden of our relationship to become even weightier. We may even discuss our annoyance with others. Then the next time we are together, our anger or displeasure wells up within us, then seeps out into our words and actions toward the other person.

In todays' verse, we are told it is to our glory (in other words, it is to our honor) to overlook the offense of another. Said differently, *"Fools show their annoyance at once, but the prudent overlook an insult"* (Prov 12:16). Pretty graphic word there: fools. Jesus also painted a shocking illustration of how to treat the injustices of others toward us when he said, *"If someone slaps you on the cheek, turn to them the other also"* (Luke 6:29). These commands give us clear direction about how we are to respond when someone offends us.

🏃 ACTION

Each time you feel wronged or offended today, make an intentional choice to overlook the offense. This does not mean denying the person's actions or words hurt you or made you angry, nor does it mean denying what he did was wrong or offensive. It does mean you are choosing to overlook what he did and cover it in grace.

You are no longer adding the offense to that mountain of offenses in your mind. When he hurts you or makes you angry, talk with God about it instead of talking about it with him or with anyone else. Pour out your heart to Jesus and tell him how it made you feel, keeping in mind the person who hurt you is also one of God's precious and treasured creations. Then ask him to help you release the wrong from your mind and your heart. You may have to talk to God about the offense multiple times in order to release it into his capable hands.

✎ **JOURNAL**

_____

_____

_____

_____

_____

_____

Wednesday

Praise the LORD, my soul; all my inmost being, praise his holy Name. Praise the LORD, my soul, and forget not all his benefits—who forgives all your sins and heals all your diseases, who redeems your life from the pit and crowns you with love and compassion, who satisfies your desires with good things so that your youth is renewed like the eagle's. The LORD works righteousness and justice for all the oppressed. He made known his ways to Moses, his deeds to the people of Israel: The LORD is compassionate and gracious, slow to anger, abounding in love. He will not always accuse, nor will he harbor his anger forever; he does not treat us as our sins deserve or repay us according to our iniquities. For as high as the heavens are above the earth, so great is his love for those who fear him; as far as the east is from the west, so far has he removed our transgressions from us. As a father has compassion on his children, so the LORD has compassion on those who fear him; for he knows how we are formed, he remembers that we are dust. (Ps 103:1–14)

IN OUR BUSY LIVES, it is easy to forget (and sometimes not even take notice at all) the extraordinary gifts the Lord lavishes on us. Yet when we choose to remember and ponder the staggering benefits we have from being in a relationship with the loving creator of the universe, it can transform our lives. When we seriously consider all he has done for us, we can develop a healthier perspective of our situations. Therefore, today the focus will not be on the earthly relationship you are working to make better, but instead it will be on how your heavenly Father treats you.

🏃 ACTION

Read the verses from Psalm 103 on the following pages and write at least one way each of them applies to you now or has in the past. Keep these benefits in mind and allow yourself to relish these gifts, basking in them and fully enjoying them. After you have written your answers, you might want to take a photo of them with your phone so you can carry them with you to help you remember them.

The Lord forgives all your sins and heals all your diseases.

_____

_____

_____

He redeems your life from the pit and crowns you with love and compassion.

_____

_____

_____

He satisfies your desires with good things so that your youth is renewed like the eagle's.

_____

_____

_____

The LORD works righteousness and justice for all the oppressed.

_____

_____

_____

He made known his ways to Moses, his deeds to the people of Israel.

_____

_____

_____

The LORD is compassionate and gracious, slow to anger, abounding in love.

_____

_____

_____

He will not always accuse, nor will he harbor his anger forever; he does not treat us as our sins deserve or repay us according to our iniquities.

_____

_____

_____

As high as the heavens are above the earth, so great is his love for those who fear him.

_____

_____

_____

As far as the east is from the west, so far has he removed our transgressions from us.

_____

_____

_____

As a father has compassion on his children, so the LORD has compassion on those who fear him.

_____

_____

_____

He knows how we are formed, he remembers that we are dust.

_____

_____

_____

✏ **JOURNAL**

_____

_____

_____

_____

_____

_____

Friday

📖 *My soul thirsts for God, for the living God. When can I go and meet with God? (Ps 42:2)*

YOU MAY HAVE HEARD the idea that no earthly relationship can satisfy the deepest longings of your heart, and that there is a place in your heart only God can fill. However, sometimes we forget this fact when we try to get all our emotional needs met from people. This tendency can put a tremendous amount of strain on our relationships. The more we attempt to have people meet the needs only God can fill, the more they are likely to feel pressured, which can cause them to withdraw from us. Their withdrawal can send us chasing after them in a desperate attempt to avoid what feels like emotional abandonment, causing them to withdraw even further, and a vicious cycle begins. To break this pattern, we must redirect our energies and attention to getting our needs filled by God. Then when our emotional tanks are full, we are in a better place to relate to all the people in our lives, including those with whom we have a challenging relationship.

🏃 ACTION

In this exercise, you will once again not be focusing on your troubled relationship, but instead you will be working on your relationship with the Lord. Plan a day within the next seven days to go somewhere and spend time with Jesus. Choose a location where you will be able to read your Bible, pray, and listen to worship music. Some possible meeting places could be a lake, a park, a coffee shop, a café, the mountains, the beach, or a church (not during regular service times). Pick a place where you can pray (even with your eyes open) without people coming up to you to talk, and a place where you enjoy being. Put some effort into imagining where you will go and meet with God, just as you would put effort into picking a place where you and a human you love might go and meet. Even if you live alone and regularly spend time with God in your home, for this assignment go somewhere else. Plan to take your Bible, a pen, this book to journal in, and a music device with you.

When you arrive, begin by inviting the Lord to be present there with you. Of course, we know God is always present, but by inviting him to be with you, you are opening your heart and mind to his presence. Your purpose during this time is to focus on loving God, to confess any sins you have, to be receptive to him, to pour out your heart to him, and to seek him to satisfy your heart's longings. Have some worship music available so you can spend some time praising him.

✏️ JOURNAL

_____

_____

_____

_____

_____

_____

Monday

📖 *The law from your mouth is more precious to me than thousands of pieces of silver and gold. (Ps 119:72)*

The law of the LORD is perfect, refreshing the soul. The statutes of the LORD are trustworthy, making wise the simple. The precepts of the LORD are right, giving joy to the heart. The commands of the LORD are radiant, giving light to the eyes. The fear of the LORD is pure, enduring forever. The decrees of the LORD are firm, and all of them are righteous. They are more precious than gold, than much pure gold; they are sweeter than honey, than honey from the honeycomb. By them your servant is warned; in keeping them there is great reward. (Ps 19:7–11)

WHEN YOU THINK ABOUT the commands and laws of God, do they give you joy? Are they more precious to you than gold? When you think about it, this is quite an extraordinary thing to love about God. I often hear Christians say they love God's grace, his mercy, or his forgiveness, but I am not sure I have ever heard anyone say how much they love God's laws, have you? Even if you do know one person who says that, why do you suppose it is so rare? My guess is because we like to focus on things that bring us instant gratification, and we probably consider the law as a restriction of our freedoms rather than something that brings us pleasure. Why then does the author of this psalm love the law and why should we aim for loving it ourselves?

The psalmist who wrote Psalm 119 describes several reasons we may not readily consider. He tells us the laws, statutes, precepts, decrees, and commands of God refresh us, make us wise, give us joy, and provide light for us to see. This an incredible gift package from God when you think about it! Who doesn't want to be refreshed, to be wise, to have joy and light to see? But how often do we consider God's laws, statues, precepts, decrees, and commands to be the supplier of those things? Viewed in this light, we can begin to see why the psalmist loved them.

In verse eleven, we learn even more about the value of following God's rules: "*By them your servant is warned; in keeping them there is great reward.*" The laws, commands, statutes, decrees, and precepts are in place to warn us to stay away from danger and to lead us toward reward. Sounds like a simple formula for motivating human behavior, doesn't it? Avoid pain, move toward pleasure. It seems this psalmist loved the law because he saw in it a straightforward plan that would make peoples' lives better if followed consistently.

Today's Action assignment is designed to help you look at the practical ways God's commands and laws impact your life and how you can grow to appreciate him for giving them to us. There are also some questions which may help you uncover any neglected commands or laws that may be negatively impacting your relationship.

𝓍 ACTION

Are there any laws, decrees, statutes, or commands you love? If so, list them here and describe what you love about them.

_____

_____

_____

Have you thanked God recently for any of his commands? Do you do this regularly?

_____

_____

_____

How do you demonstrate your love for the laws and commands you listed in the relationship in which you are struggling?

_____

_____

_____

Are there any commands or laws that you have chosen to overlook because you do not want to do them in your relationship?

_____

_____

_____

If yes, which ones?

_____

_____

_____

What would be some of the potential rewards for obeying the commands you have overlooked?

_____

_____

_____

What might be some pitfalls you could avoid by heeding their warnings?

_____

_____

_____

How can you begin to love God's laws and commands better?

_____

_____

_____

✎ JOURNAL

_____

_____

_____

_____

_____

_____

Wednesday

Live in harmony with one another . . . if it is possible, as far as it depends on you, live at peace with everyone. (Rom 12:16, 18)

WHEN YOU THINK OF the term "harmony," what comes to mind? When I think of this word, I think of music and the way voices and instruments blend to make a beautiful sound. If I visualize this term in connection with healthy relationships, I envision people smiling at each other, laughing together, heads nodding in agreement as they take turns speaking, and a sense of peace and restfulness. Chances are, though, when you picture the relationship(s) with which you are struggling, instead of picturing harmony you probably see discord.

The verses in Romans 12 indicate the importance God places on his children getting along well with each other, and they provide an important directive: as far as it depends on you, live at peace with everyone. Notice in verse eighteen where the responsibility rests: *on you.*

At first, you may think it is unfair you should have to shoulder the responsibility for trying to make peace considering how badly he treats you. However, this is an immensely powerful position in which God places his children. What I mean is it is much better to be able to take responsibility for trying to make peace than to wait on someone else to do it. In fact, Psalm 34:14 tells us we are to *"seek peace and pursue it."* Do you see the active engagement and personal responsibility this verse requires? We are not just to hope peace will come to our relationship; we are to go after it.

∗ ACTION

Begin by closing your eyes and imagine being with the person whose relationship you want to make better. Picture yourself smiling warmly as you greet him (it's incredible how much body language plays a role in the success or breakdown of our relationships), see yourself shaking your head in agreement with something he says, picture yourself laughing with him in a lighthearted way. Think ahead to a conversation you might be having the next time you see him and what you can say to create harmony.

You will also want to prepare for ways you can steer away from any topic you know could lead to a disagreement. Since you have probably been in this relationship for a while, you know where the minefields are, so stay clear of them! If he brings up something that is a sore subject, think of things you can say to bring back harmony. For example, you might say something like, "I understand what you're saying. That's an important point and I would like to think more about it and talk about it with you later today." This will give you time to think about your response to a difficult subject, and hopefully you will be able to come up with some new "harmonious" ways to handle the matter you have not considered in the past.

Spend a few moments now mentally rehearsing these harmonious images and dialogue in your mind, then repeat this a few of times before you will be together.

✏ JOURNAL

_____

_____

_____

_____

_____

_____

Friday

- Make a conscious effort to overlook offenses.
- Remember how God treats you and the benefits you have from being in a relationship with him.
- Recall what you experienced with the Lord the day you went away and met with him.
- Think about how you can love the commands of the Lord more.
- Think of a harmonious conversation you had with the person whose relationship you are working to make better.
- Are you praying daily for your relationship?

JOURNAL

_____

_____

_____

_____

_____

_____

Monday

📖 *He does not treat us as our sins deserve or repay us according to our iniquities. (Ps 13:10)*

Do not say, "I'll do to them as they have done to me; I'll pay them back for what they did." (Prov 24:29)

Do not take revenge, my dear friends, but leave room for God's wrath, for it is written: "It is mine to avenge; I will repay," says the Lord. (Rom 12:19)

HUMANS WERE MADE BY God and in his image: "*So God created mankind in his own image, in the image of God he created them; male and female he created them*" (Gen 1:27). However, although God's character is perfect, our character is flawed which means we do not perfectly reflect his image (now tell you something you didn't know, right?).

One example of how we imperfectly reflect God's attributes is in the area of justice. Our God is a just God who desires justice in his Kingdom: "*The LORD is known by his acts of justice; the wicked are ensnared by the work of their hands*" (Ps 9:16); "*The LORD loves righteousness and justice; the earth is full of his unfailing love*" (Ps 33:5); "*And the heavens proclaim his righteousness, for he is a God of justice*" (Ps 50:6). Because we reflect his image, we, too, desire to see justice done in our lives and in the lives of others. When we see a wrong being committed, there is a sense we have that something should be done to correct the wrong, which in and of itself is good. The problem comes when we decide we should be the one to be the judge, jury, and executioner.

When we are in a relationship filled with tension, we are likely to become hypersensitive to any infractions committed against us. Our emotional radar may be set to an ultra-high level to detect incoming insults to guard ourselves from further harm. Then, because we have this inborn sense of justice, we desire to seek "justice" and make things "right." However, because we are so focused on the other person's wrongs, we are often blinded to the role we might be playing in the situation.

In his kindness to us, God has made allowance for our unbalanced sense of justice. What is his solution? He has told us to leave any payback we believe we are due in his hands and to let him take care of it. Does this mean we are never to take action against sin? No. In fact, the Bible tells us one way we can address the sin of another in Matthew 18:15–20, which we will discuss on another day. The point is, God wants us to let him be the ultimate Judge and to entrust our wounds into his healing hands.

𝓡 ACTION

You probably can easily come up with several wrongs/sins/offenses the person with whom you are struggling has committed against you without a lot of thought. Those offenses may sit just below the surface of your consciousness or may even be right in the forefront of your mind.

While I am writing this, I am thinking about the burden you may be suffering from these sins you have endured. I know for most of you who are reading this, the offenses may have felt like they were tearing your heart out. What's worse, chances are there have been *multiple* times the person has committed those offenses and many others against you. I want you to know I do not take lightly the wrongdoings you have had to endure, and it is with great sensitivity to your pain I offer this opportunity to begin healing from these wounds. But remember, because these wounds are probably old and deep, it may feel like you have just scratched the surface with this assignment, and that is ok. You are taking a positive step toward healing.

To help you begin to turn over to God the wrongs the person has done to you, on a separate sheet of paper write down some of the things that have hurt you deeply. As you look at your list, remind yourself you trust Jesus to do the right thing to establish justice in your life (after all, he has established justice for all the nations, therefore, he can certainly do this for you). Next, pray and ask God to help you let these things go to him once and for all. Confess how you have been carrying these hurtful thoughts and feelings, but now you want to be free of their weighty burden. Finally, tear the paper into tiny fragments and imagine placing the shreds of paper into God's hands. While doing this, thank him for taking these matters out of your hands and into his own perfectly just and powerful hands. (When you are finished with this exercise, thoroughly dispose of the fragments of paper so no one will find them. You do not want to harm the relationship you are working so very hard to heal). The next time these offenses come to mind, remind yourself you have turned them over to God.

✐ **JOURNAL**

Wednesday

And now, dear brothers and sisters, one final thing. Fix your thoughts on what is true, and honorable, and right, and pure, and lovely, and admirable. Think about things that are excellent and worthy of praise. (Phil 4:8)

THE IMPORTANCE OF WHAT we think about cannot be overestimated, which is why I have spent several lessons thus far on the topic of our thought content. Today we are once again going to focus on replacing negative thoughts with those outlined in today's verse.

Far too often, I find myself thinking about the negative things in life. If I am honest, I do not always naturally turn my attention to what is true, honorable, pure, lovely, admirable, excellent, or praiseworthy. In fact, I think it is often just the opposite. It is almost as if my mind is determined to seek out lies, to find fault, and to focus on negative details instead of looking for what is good and decent. When it comes to our challenging relationships, this negative pattern of thinking can dominate our thoughts. Fortunately, God understands this tendency in us, and he has a remedy for it: he tells us to take hold of our thoughts and intentionally focus on the good.

✝ ACTION

To help reorient your thoughts about the person whose relationship you want to make better, write one adjective in each oval from Philippians 4:8 describing some of his positive qualities on the bookmark on page 97. After you have finished, cut out the paper and then use it as a bookmark or leave it laying around where you will see it often throughout the days. Whenever your thoughts turn negative, refocus your attention on those positive qualities he possesses.

✏ JOURNAL

_____

_____

_____

_____

_____

_____

Friday

When they came to the place called the Skull, they crucified him there, along with the criminals—one on his right, the other on his left. Jesus said, "Father, forgive them, for they do not know what they are doing." (Luke 23:33–34)

ONE OF THE CENTRAL tenets of Christianity is forgiveness. When we think about the attributes of God which we are to model after him, right at the top of the list would be the ability to forgive anyone of anything since he has done that very thing for us by sacrificing his Son.

The supernatural ability of God's children to forgive amazes me. For example, one year I had the extraordinary opportunity of traveling to Rwanda on a mission trip while I was working on my doctorate. A group of us who were working on our degrees were given the opportunity to help the people who had suffered through the Rwandan Genocide of 1994. If you are unfamiliar with this tragedy, it was a bloody, one-hundred-day massacre of people turning against their fellow citizens. In the end, almost one million people were killed by the cruelest methods imaginable, and many more were raped and mutilated. Those who lived through it say it was truly a hell on earth.

I will never forget the day I was sitting under a straw-thatched roof in a remote village with nineteen other students seated beside me. We listened with shock and horror to people describe what it was like to live through that killing rampage. Tears came to one woman's eyes when she recounted how her family was savagely murdered by a man who had been her neighbor all her life. We all sat in rapt attention as she told the grotesque way her family was butchered; but then something incredible happened.

She introduced a man who had been standing off to the side when she was telling her story. The man came forward slowly as she motioned for him to stand next to her. As he stood there, she told us this man had been one of the murderers! A sense of fear jolted through me as I realized I was within a few feet of the person whose monstrous acts of murder had just been so vividly portrayed. As I looked at the two of them standing together and listened to her words, I began to understand why she was no longer afraid of him, and why he was a man who was no longer intent on murder and mayhem.

The woman told us how, after some sense of order had been restored to Rwanda, a pastor whose family had also been brutally murdered began walking through the land preaching the Good News of Jesus to all who would listen. Among those who heard this news were the man and woman who stood before us that day. The man had repented of his evil deeds during those dark days and began to demonstrate his changed attitude by doing things for the woman to show his contrition. One of the things he did to try to make amends was to build her and her surviving children a home.

As you can imagine, the pain of losing her family was still with the woman, but she was able to forgive him by the power of God despite what he had done. What was even more incredible was how her forgiveness had born itself out in her life: she allowed him to take care of her children sometimes while she was busy gathering food and water! Yes, she left this murderous (but repentant) man alone with her two precious children because God had brought her to a place of true forgiveness.

When I think about the situations in which I must forgive people who have harmed me, they pale in comparison to what I witnessed in Rwanda. It is not that the sins others have committed against me are minor. In fact, some of the offenses of others toward me have been extremely damaging and painful and have had lifelong consequences. But the fact is, no matter how much others may have harmed me, I have never suffered what the Rwandans suffered at the hands of their perpetrators, or a thousand other sins people have endured at the hands of evil doers. When I put this knowledge in the context of Christianity, I remember Jesus's decision to forgive those who were crucifying him. What Jesus did on the cross and the ways others have forgiven their perpetrators inspires me to allow forgiveness to permeate all my relationships, whether or not the people are repentant.

🏃 ACTION

This Action assignment has two parts. In the first part, picture in your mind today's verses and thank Jesus for his sacrifice. Then search your heart to see if there is any unforgiveness toward the person whose relationship you are working on and confess it to God. Ask him to give you the power to forgive the way he forgave others and the way he has forgiven you.

For the second part of the assignment, you will select a movie to watch about forgiveness. There are many excellent movies that can help motivate us to forgive when we see the model of others. Here are a few examples, but feel free to choose something different:

- *Forgiving Dr. Mengele*
- *I Can Only Imagine*
- *Unbroken* (*and its sequel*) *Unbroken: Path to Redemption*
- *End of the Spear*

✎ JOURNAL

_____

_____

_____

_____

_____

_____

Monday

> But I trust in You, LORD; I say, "You are my God." My times are in your hands. (Ps 31:14–15)

Rejoice in the Lord always. I will say it again: Rejoice! (Phil 4:4)

IT IS NOT UNUSUAL for people to experience a great deal of fear and anxiety when dealing with a challenging relationship, and perhaps you have experienced this yourself. If left unattended, these emotional responses can push you to make fear-based instead of faith-based choices, which in turn can create an entirely new set of problems to deal with in the relationship. Thankfully, you do not have to allow fear to rule your life, but instead you can live in faith, trust, and peace. The two verses for today complement each other because they both can provide a helpful and powerful focus for your thoughts when you are anxious or afraid. Instead of being fearful, you can choose to trust in God. Since you have a God in whom you can trust, you can rejoice instead of worry.

Often when we feel anxious or afraid, we are not even aware why we have a vague feeling of apprehension, but we nonetheless feel it. Whether we realize it or not, our minds are never completely idle: we are always thinking about something. During the times when you are feeling anxious, it is important to stop and pay attention to your thoughts. Once you know what you are thinking, you can take control of the thoughts by replacing them with something constructive from Scripture. For example, when you find yourself consumed with fear or anxiety, examine your thoughts and then remind yourself to think about God who is a loving, all-powerful, all-knowing Father worthy of your trust. Or you can choose to remember Jesus has promised he will never leave you or forsake you (Heb 13:5). You can replace your anxious thoughts with any Scriptures that are comforting to you.

This may seem like a simple solution to dealing with fear and anxiety, doesn't it? I understand there are times when anxiety becomes so unmanageable a person may need to seek help from a counselor and when that is the case, a wise biblical counselor can help bring about remarkable healing. However, it is important to note counselors often focus on helping people identify their thoughts and then they work with them to change harmful thought patterns. Therefore, in many cases, people can alleviate or even heal their own anxiety by consistently paying attention to their thoughts, and then changing them to line up with God's word.

🏃 ACTION

If you have a smart phone, program into your calendar a daily or twice daily alert reminding you to check your thoughts and then to reorder them based on verses that are comforting to you. For example, you could set your alert for noon every day to read something like, "What am I thinking about right now?" *"But I trust in You, LORD; I say, 'You are my God. My times are in Your hands'"* (Ps 31:14–15). Alternatively, you could have a couple of different verses appear at two set times every day. You could set one for when you are getting ready in the morning, and then perhaps another one right after lunch. You know when your energy tends to be low every day or when you are vulnerable to being anxious, so choose times that will be the most effective for you. When the reminder goes off, take a moment to be alert to what you are thinking, and then redirect your focus to scriptural truths instead of the cares of this world.

JOURNAL

_____

_____

_____

_____

_____

_____

Wednesday

📖 *Take my yoke upon you and learn from me, for I am gentle and humble in heart, and you will find rest for your souls. (Matt 11:29)*

Be completely humble and gentle; be patient, bearing with one another in love. (Eph 4:2)

Therefore, as God's chosen people, holy and dearly loved, clothe yourselves with compassion, kindness, humility, gentleness, and patience. (Col 3:12)

Remind the people . . . always to be gentle toward everyone. (Titus 3:1, 2)

But the fruit of the Spirit is love, joy, peace, forbearance, kindness, goodness, faithfulness, gentleness, and self-control. (Gal 5:22–23)

Blessed are the meek (gentle) for they will inherit the earth. (Matt 5:5)

Your beauty should not come from outward adornment, such as elaborate hairstyles and the wearing of gold jewelry or fine clothes. Rather, it should be that of your inner self, the unfading beauty of a gentle and quiet spirit, which is of great worth in God's sight. (1 Pet 3:3–4)

ARE YOU FAMILIAR WITH the expression "like a bull in a China shop?" It refers to people who are careless or brash in the way they speak or how they move. Contrast that with the expression "as gentle as a lamb," which describes people who are mild-mannered and calm. If you had to choose between those two expressions, how would you describe yourself? Are you more of a lamb or a bull when it comes to how you interact with the person with whom you have a challenging relationship?

The verses for today all contain the term *gentle*. *Merriam Webster* dictionary defines gentle as being "free from harshness, sternness, or violence."[1] It is important to note being gentle does not mean lacking power, after all, the Bible says Jesus is gentle. Therefore, a gentle person can possess great power but wield it without being harsh or abrasive.

When you think about the people with whom you get along well, you probably picture those people who are most often gentle toward you. But what if your personality is more like a bull than a lamb? This can create quite a challenge to be gentle in your day-to-day life, especially with those who irritate or upset you. Fortunately, God does not expect you to produce characteristics of the Fruit of the Spirit (see Gal 5:22–23 above) on your own. He has given you the ability to have and display these attributes when you draw upon his supernatural power. You may be wondering how to draw upon this power within you, so I will describe how this works.

When you accepted Jesus as your Savior, the Holy Spirit entered your heart (if you have not accepted Jesus as your Savior, please see the back of this book for information about how to be saved on the page entitled "The Plan of Salvation"). At the time of your new birth, the Holy Spirit came to live in you, and it was not just part of the Holy Spirit but all of him who indwelt you. What this means is from the time you were born again, the same power that rose Jesus from the grave took residence in your life and made himself and his power available to you: *"I pray that the eyes of your heart may be enlightened in order that you may know the hope to which he has called you, the riches of his glorious inheritance in his*

---

1. *Merriam Webster*, "Gentle."

holy people, and his incomparably great power for us who believe. That power is the same as the mighty strength he exerted when he raised Christ from the dead and seated him at his right hand in the heavenly realms" (Eph 1:18–20). Those are power-filled verses! Please go back and read them again. The trouble is we do not always draw upon that power.

In order to use the power the Holy Spirit provides during difficult encounters, we must first take our focus off the other person and identify the emotional reactions going on within ourselves. After we identify our thoughts and emotions, we can look to the Holy Spirit within us to guide us regardless of how we are feeling or what we are thinking. Not only will he give us guidance, he will also give us his strength and power in exchange for our weakness to help us carry out his will.

🏃 ACTION

Pray and ask God to show you how to respond gently ahead of those times when you may find yourself in a difficult situation. If you wait until the moment a problem arises, you will likely revert to old ways of responding. After God reveals the type of response you are to have, ask him to empower you when you are weak. Have a Scripture from today's verses about gentleness memorized so the Holy Spirit can bring it to your memory when the moment of testing comes. Finally, the next time you are feeling provoked, listen to the Holy Spirit within you and do not overlook his prompting. You will know it is the Holy Spirit because his direction will line up 100% with his word. Even though your human nature will want to give into your old ways of responding, don't do it! Respond with gentleness and remember that following God will move you down the path of healing you desire in your relationship.

✎ JOURNAL

_____

_____

_____

_____

_____

_____

Friday

↩ REVIEW

- Be sure you continue not to hold onto those offenses you turned over to God.

- Look over the bookmark you made and reflect on the other person's positive qualities.

- Remember the sacrifice of Christ and his willingness to forgive you as well as the examples of how others have forgiven evils committed against them.

- If needed, adjust the times your phone notifies you to set your focus on trusting God and rejoicing in him so they are most beneficial to you.

- Are you looking to God to empower you to express the Fruit of the Spirit in all circumstances?

- Are you praying daily for your relationship?

✏ JOURNAL

_____

_____

_____

_____

_____

_____

Monday

📖 *Confess your faults to one another and pray for one another that you may be healed. (Jas 5:16)*

SOME OF THE GREATEST experiences I have had with the Lord were during times when I asked other people to pray for me. I remember occasions when I felt desperate for relief from pressing temptations and nothing I did seemed to help until I shared my struggle with a friend and that person prayed for me. Those encounters powerfully showed me God's supernatural working to free me from temptations I could not escape on my own. Today's verse teaches us an important principle: we can receive healing from God when we confess our sin to someone and receive prayer in exchange.

A word of caution is needed as you apply this verse. It is important to be aware of what it is not telling us to do. We are not told to share with someone the faults of the person with whom we are struggling. In other words, we are not told to gossip about the sins another person is committing or has committed against us. Although we can sometimes gain prayer and often sympathy when we do that, it is sin and sin only brings destruction. I am not saying you can never share with someone what is happening in your relationship *if your purpose for sharing is to receive godly counsel so you can find a biblical way to handle the situation.* That is very different from gossip. What this verse is telling us to do is to share our own shortcomings with someone who will be faithful to pray for us and we are to do the same for others.

If you are in a situation where sin is weighing heavily upon you, know you are not alone. Do not let the enemy of your soul (Satan) lead you to believe you are the only one who has ever done what you are doing or have done because that is a lie. We have all had sin we were ashamed of and were afraid if anyone knew about it they would abandon us, humiliate us before others, stop loving us, ridicule, or judge us. We have all sinned and fallen short of the glory of God (Rom 3:23), but God wants to forgive you and give you freedom from your sin.

🏃 ACTION

If there is sin in your life with which you are struggling, pray and ask God for discernment about whether he would have you talk with someone you trust about it. If you sense God leading you to do this, do not let shame, fear, pride, or anything else keep you from receiving the healing you need. When you choose someone to share your burden with, make sure the person is a strong, prayerful Christian who you can trust to keep the matter between the two of you. After the person prays for you, offer to do the same for him.

✏ JOURNAL

_____

_____

_____

_____

_____

_____

Wednesday

📖 *No king is saved by the multitude of an army; a mighty man is not delivered by his great strength. (Ps 33:16)*

In your hands are strength and power to exalt and give strength to all. (1 Chr 29:12)

IN THE WESTERN WORLD, we pride ourselves on our independence. We lavish praise and honor on people when they rise out of the ashes by their cunning, strength, and internal fortitude. I live in the great state of Texas where we are especially inclined to revere and promote independence. The silhouetted figure of a cowboy on the open range battling the forces of nature and carving out an existence by himself is venerated here.

Although we rejoice in our independence, it can actually be a disadvantage when viewed from a biblical perspective. Although humans tend to prize self-sufficiency, God values our dependence on him. An illustration of this is found in 1 Samuel 16.

In this passage of Scripture, we find the story of David and King Saul. The Bible tells us Saul was afraid of David because he knew God was with David, and he knew God had left him because of his disobedience. We also learn Saul was jealous of David because David was more successful than he was in leading military campaigns. Furthermore, Saul was jealous because the people of his own kingdom loved and praised David. Saul was so jealous of David he eventually even tried to kill him!

Knowing Saul's determination to kill him, if David had relied on his own strengths or resources, he might have considered mounting a political campaign against Saul to bring him down. After all, in 1 Samuel 18:3–4 we learn David had a close relationship with Saul's son Jonathan. Jonathan had turned his allegiance away from his own father and given it instead to David. Therefore, David could have taken advantage of that loyalty by joining forces with Jonathan to take his rightful place as the successor king. But that is not what David did. David also had a powerful army that had resulted in many successful battles under his command which he could have used to wage war against Saul. David did not do that either. We also find in 1 Samuel 22:2 David had a faithful fan base who, if he had told them how Saul had been treating him, could have been incited to revolt against Saul. This, however, was not how David responded. We are even shown a time in 1 Samuel 24:1–10 when David had the chance to retaliate against Saul by killing him, but David chose to walk away from that opportunity. Even with all these resources and opportunities at his disposal, David did not choose to draw upon any of them. Instead, his response was to treat Saul consistently with kindness and respect, regardless of how Saul treated him. David's other method for dealing with Saul was to regularly appeal to God for deliverance. Notice where David sought relief: from God.

I would imagine it is unlikely you have the same kind of resources David did when he was dealing with his extremely difficult relationship with Saul. However, I know you do have resources you can draw upon, some of which you may have already been using to try to deal with your relationship. Perhaps you have many friends with whom you can pour out your heart, which makes you feel better . . . for a time. Or maybe you have financial resources that allow you to cover the pain of your relationship by buying things to make yourself feel better . . . for a time. Maybe you have a great job you can focus on so you do not have to deal with the stress of your relationship . . . for a time. But let me ask you, are you appealing to God for his mighty power on your behalf daily? Are you admitting and agreeing with the Lord you are powerless to change the other person and it is only by his help you will ever gain any ground in having a more satisfying relationship?

🏃 ACTION

We are often unaware of the ways we relate to people, especially with those we find difficult to handle. It is as though we have blind spots (notice the term blind *spots*, not blind spot—you get the idea) about how to have a healthy relationship. Therefore, today's Action is designed to help you uncover some ways you may be relying on your own strengths and resources in your current relationship.

Ask yourself the following questions: (1) Do I demand he treat me the way I would like to be treated, or do I regularly ask God for help with this? (2) Do I give him the silent treatment, withhold affection, or some other form of emotional or physical "punishment" to make him respond the way I want him to respond? (3) Do I tell my friends/family how he is treating me instead of talking it over with God? (4) Do I avoid dealing with the relationship by immersing myself in activities such as shopping/eating/drinking/working instead of immersing myself in prayer over him, the relationship, and myself? (5) Do I treat him with respect and humbly submit myself into God's mighty hands, or do I treat him the way he treats me? If you answered any of these questions in a manner that shows your reliance is on your own inner strengths or resources, there is a simple (although not necessarily easy) way to begin to move out of this pattern. Although this may seem like a small step, it requires a giant leap of faith.

Begin by humbly confessing to God your reliance upon yourself. Ask for his forgiveness for not relying upon and trusting in him and in his power to help you with this relationship. Perhaps you may also need to confess how it is somewhat unsettling for you to leave this relationship entirely in the Lord's hands. In other words, you may not be able to trust God fully with this relationship right now because you have always relied on yourself. If that is the case, confess it to God and say something to him like, *"Lord, I believe; help my unbelief"* (Mark 9:23). Lastly, commit to memory one of the verses in this section that will help you remember from where your help will come. When you notice you are relying on your old methods, recite the verse to yourself, confess, and ask again for God's aid. Then step back and watch for ways God is working.

✎ JOURNAL

_____

_____

_____

_____

_____

_____

Friday

"If your brother or sister sins, go and point out their fault, just between the two of you. If they listen to you, you have won them over. But if they will not listen, take one or two others along, so that 'every matter may be established by the testimony of two or three witnesses.' If they still refuse to listen, tell it to the church; and if they refuse to listen even to the church, treat them as you would a pagan or a tax collector. Truly I tell you, whatever you bind on earth will be bound in heaven, and whatever you loose on earth will be loosed in heaven. Again, truly I tell you that if two of you on earth agree about anything they ask for, it will be done for them by my Father in heaven. For where two or three gather in my Name, there am I with them." (Matt 18:15–20)

As I DISCUSSED ON previous days, it is often necessary to overlook the offenses of others and/or to leave justice in the hands of God. The Bible discusses both practices as necessary for maintaining relationships that are pleasing to him. But the Bible also describes situations in which sin should be addressed and not overlooked, and the verses in Matthew 18:15–20 portray a very specific way God wants this to be done.

Before we look in detail at the method outlined in Matthew, let's first get some clarity about what kind of sin might be dealt with in this manner. As you can see from these verses, this is a serious method that could ultimately end up in the hands of the church where a person could be ostracized from fellowship. Therefore, we want to be sure we take this seriously. Because of the gravity of this course of action, not every sin should be handled this way. In most situations, we can address the sins of others and move on and/or apply the verses I covered in weeks 3 and 5. However, when we sense we may need to do more, God has provided us with detailed plans about how to proceed.

The first step in knowing if a sin falls into this category is prayer. We cannot know if a sin should be discussed with the offender or overlooked without first taking the matter to God. Since this passage is speaking only to Christians (both the offender and the offended must be Christian for these verses to apply), both people are God's precious and cherished saints who should be treated with love and respect as co-heirs of salvation. If you find yourself in a situation where you are considering taking action, go to God first and pour out your heart to him. Although we know God is omnipresent (everywhere) and omniscient (all knowing), he still wants us to talk things over with him and receive his guidance. Let him know how you have been harmed by the sin and ask him if you should take the matter to the person who offended you. Then wait for his answer. Waiting is key. Give God time to reveal his heart to you about the issue. Sometimes God will work in the other person's heart and the person will repent without you saying anything. Sometimes God will have you go to that person and point out his sin. At other times, God may have you drop the matter entirely. It is only by going to God in prayer and waiting upon his response that you will know how to proceed.

If after praying about the issue you believe God is leading you to approach the offender, let's examine the biblical method to correctly deal with the situation. Beginning in verse fifteen we are told, "*If your brother or sister sins, go and point out their fault, just between the two of you.*" The solution is quite simple (although not always easy): go to him and tell him his sin when the two of you are alone together. The way you approach and speak to him should be the way God wants you to treat him on every occasion: with humility, kindness, compassion, gentleness, and love, remembering you, too, have fallen into sin countless times in your life. There should be no screaming or yelling, no put-downs, sarcasm, or finger pointing. You are to show him his fault then stop. If he listens to you, the Bible indicates that means you have won him over. The matter is then closed, and you are not to keep a record of this wrong because love "*. . . keeps no record of wrongs*" (1 Cor 13: 5) no matter how "big" of a sin it was.

But what if he will not listen? The next step in that case is to "*take one or two others along, so that 'every matter may be established by the testimony of two or three witnesses'*" (Matt 18:16). The Bible does not specify what kind of people you should take with you, but my belief is it should be people who are spiritually minded and who you can trust to keep this between the three or four of you. The point is to have someone else point out the error to the brother so he will have a change of heart. Again, if he listens the matter is resolved, and the case is closed. But what if he still will not listen?

"*If they still refuse to listen, tell it to the church*" (Matt 18:17). I believe your next step would be to take this to your pastor. If your church has a process for church discipline, your pastor will lead the way. Then, if necessary, the final step of ostracizing the brother from the fellowship will occur.

In Matthew 18:18–20, God declared a solemn announcement letting everyone know if this procedure is followed and the believer still will not listen, he will have bound in Heaven the agreement the church has bound on earth. Stop and think about this a moment. This is so serious God has joined together with the church and made it official in Heaven. The verses following this declaration from God are often taken out of context and put into situations where they do not belong, so let's read them in the context of this procedure on dealing with a brother in sin who will not listen to the church's rebuke. "*Again, truly I tell you that if two of you on earth agree about anything they ask for, it will be done for them by my Father in heaven. For where two or three gather in my*

Name, there am I with them." Here, God is specifically addressing what has happened in the church when a brother is ostracized from fellowship.

🏃 ACTION

If you are considering beginning the procedure outlined in Matthew 18 with a brother who has sinned against you, these verses should make you shudder with fear with what is at stake. If they do not, it is possible you are not ready to move forward because you have not considered the gravity of this course of action. Before moving ahead, please go back to my first admonition in this section which was to spend time in prayer and wait upon the Lord for his direction.

If you are awe-struck over the enormity of these verses and their implication yet you believe this is what the Lord would have you do, do so with humility and great care. God is with you as you travel his path for dealing with a brother who has sinned.

✏ JOURNAL

_____
_____
_____
_____
_____
_____

Monday

📖 *I will instruct you and teach you in the way you should go; I will counsel you with my loving eye on you. Do not be like the horse or the mule, which have no understanding but must be controlled by bit and bridle or they will not come to you. (Ps 32:8–9)*

Are not two sparrows sold for a penny? Yet not one of them will fall to the ground outside your Father's will. (Matt 10:29)

And even the very hairs of your head are all numbered. (Matt 10:30)

WOULD IT SURPRISE YOU to learn God desires to lead you in every area of your life? Today's verses teach us two important concepts about God's ways with his children. First, God did not place you on this earth to try to figure out things for yourself: he wants to teach you and guide you along the paths he has for you. Second, he cares about every detail of your life. In other words, there is not one thing about your life that is unimportant to him.

Now I know not everyone believes this. Some people believe certain things in life are too small for God to be concerned about. They believe he is busy running the universe, so they assume he expects us to figure out and handle some things on our own. With that line of reasoning, the question that comes to my mind is, where does God draw the line about what is important enough to bring to him and what is too insignificant? The truth is the Bible gives us story after story about how God desires to help us with everything in our lives. Let me give you an example to illustrate how no detail escapes God's attention, and how he desires to help us with even the smallest matters.

> *The company of the prophets said to Elisha, "Look, the place where we meet with you is too small for us. Let us go to the Jordan, where each of us can get a pole; and let us build a place there for us to meet." And he said, "Go." Then one of them said, "Won't you please come with your servants?" "I will," Elisha replied. And he went with them. They went to the Jordan and began to cut down trees. As one of them was cutting down a tree, the iron ax head fell into the water. "Oh no, my lord!" he cried out. "It was borrowed!" The man of God asked, "Where did it fall?" When he showed him the place, Elisha cut a stick and threw it there, and made the iron float. "Lift it out," he said. Then the man reached out his hand and took it* (2 Kgs 6:1–7).

In this story, we learn God even cared about a man's ax head and he performed the miraculous intervention of making it float so he could find it!

Another example of God's endless involvement in the earth he created is in Psalm 104:21: "*The lions roar for their prey and seek their food from God.*" If God cares for the day-to-day needs of the lions, he is certainly willing and able to care for all the details in your life (for more incredible examples of God's intimate involvement in the world, I encourage you to read all of Psalm 104). These examples and today's verses in Matthew 10 give us assurance we can, and in fact should, go to God for everything.

There is an important point we also need to be aware of when it comes to receiving God's instruction and aid. In Psalm 32:9 the Bible tells us, "*Do not be like the horse or the mule, which have no understanding but must be controlled by bit and bridle or they will not come to you.*" The picture painted in this verse is one of a horse who has a bit in its mouth and a bridle attached to it. If you are not familiar with how this works, the bridle attaches to the horse's head, which in turn attaches to the bit. The bit guides the horse by pulling on its mouth to make it turn one way or another, and the bit itself is controlled by reigns the rider pulls. The analogy for humans is in order to receive God's direction and assistance we should not wait until he has to put something unpleasant in our lives to steer us to him. God wants us to go to him for everything and ask for his guidance and direction. Unlike earthly parents who want their children eventually to become independent, the heavenly Father wants his children to grow in their dependence upon him.

𝍅 ACTION

Sometimes we are unfamiliar with the theological positions we hold, nonetheless those positions strongly influence important areas of our relationship with God. Today's Action is designed to help you uncover and clarify what you believe about God's availability, his willingness to come to your aid, and his desire to give you guidance. Ask yourself the following questions and then write your answers in the section below.

1. What area(s) of your relationship are you holding back from God because you think it is (they are) too small for him?

_____

_____

_____

2. Are you going to God daily and asking for his wisdom about how to handle your challenging relationship?

_____

_____

_____

3. Do you go to God willingly for help and instruction, or does something difficult have to happen before you seek his aid?

_____

_____

_____

4. What do you believe about God's willingness to help you with every detail of your life? Can you support your beliefs with Scripture?

_____

_____

_____

5. Are there any adjustments you should consider based on your last answer?

_____

_____

_____

6. Are you praying daily for your relationship?

_____

_____

_____

✏ **JOURNAL**

_____

_____

_____

_____

_____

Wednesday

And we know that in all things God works for the good of those who love him, who have been called according to his purpose. (Rom 8:28)

WHEN IN A CHALLENGING relationship, over time you are likely to experience a sense of loss in one or more areas of your life. For example, if the other person is your spouse, you may feel you have been denied the daily companionship, support, friendship, and intimacy you believe marriage should entail. If the other person is a co-worker, you may feel the loss of having a safe and serene place of work to go to every day. If the relationship is with your child, you may feel a sense of loss over your dreams for what the relationship would look like. Whatever the nature of your relationship, if it is tumultuous or unhappy you will feel deprived over certain benefits you believe should have been a part of it.

When the difficulties in your relationship began, you were probably able to let the losses go because you were hopeful things would get better soon. You probably thought the losses would be repaired, or at the very least they would eventually stop. Now, however, as the months and perhaps even years have passed by, you may be convinced you will never be able to regain what was taken from you.

Would it help you to know everything that has come to you has been filtered through God's loving hands? Let's take a moment to look at a story from the Bible to help explain this important principle.

You may be familiar with the story of Joseph in the book of Genesis (think of Joseph's coat of many colors). Joseph was the youngest son of Jacob, and he was his father's favorite. Unfortunately, Jacob did not hide his favoritism, and his brothers hated him for it (word to the wise: do not have favorites among your children!). The tensions grew between Joseph and his brothers to the point where Joseph's brothers plotted to kill him (Gen 37:18). They ended up compromising on their plan to take his life and instead sold him into slavery to a group of foreigners. Eventually, he was sold again to one of the king's officials named Potiphar.

Let's take a moment to look at Joseph's losses thus far in this story. When Joseph's brothers took him captive and sold him, he lost everything he had ever known: his home, his family, his good lifestyle, and his respected family heritage. We should not gloss over his staggering losses. Imagine being sold to strangers by your own brothers! Furthermore, try to envision what it would be like to be taken hostage to a foreign land where you do not know the customs, the language, or the culture, and then being forced into slavery. But the losses in Joseph's life did not stop there.

While Joseph was serving as a slave to Potiphar, his wife became interested in Joseph. Well, to be frank, to say she was interested in Joseph is an understatement: she lusted after Joseph. Day after day, she pursued him trying to entice him to sleep with her, but Joseph flatly refused. This enraged her and she eventually falsely accused him of trying to rape her. When Potiphar found out, he threw Joseph in prison, and that is where he remained for several years.

As you can see, Joseph's losses over all this time were staggering. In addition to the losses he experienced with his family, he then lost his freedom when he was put in prison. Keep in mind Joseph was sent to prison unjustly while he was doing his job well, being obedient to God, and not giving into temptation with Potiphar's wife.

After several years had passed, the king of Egypt had a dream that troubled him greatly. Not only could he not interpret it, neither could any of the wise men who worked for him. One of the king's servants remembered Joseph had correctly interpreted a dream for him two years prior, and he encouraged the king to seek Joseph's interpretation for his dream. When Joseph was brought before Pharaoh, he immediately gave credit to God for the ability to interpret dreams, and then proceeded to give Pharaoh the correct interpretation. The king was so impressed with Joseph's supernatural ability, he put him in charge of all Egypt! In Genesis 41:41–44, we read how it happened:

> *So Pharaoh said to Joseph, "I hereby put you in charge of the whole land of Egypt." Then Pharaoh took his signet ring from his finger and put it on Joseph's finger. He dressed him in robes of fine linen and put a gold chain around his neck. He had him ride in a chariot as his second-in-command, and people shouted before him, "Make way!" Thus, he put him in charge of the whole land of Egypt. Then Pharaoh said to Joseph, "I am Pharaoh, but without your word no one will lift hand or foot in all Egypt."*

This obviously was an incredible turn of events for Joseph. He went from being a prisoner to overseeing all of Egypt! But what about all the losses Joseph endured prior to getting to this amazing point in his life? Were these losses still part of him? Yes, they were. Just because Joseph's life had taken an incredible turn for the good does not mean all his previous suffering was forgotten. What Joseph does with those losses is where the crux of the lesson for today lies.

In Genesis 50:20–21, we learn how Joseph viewed his losses when he spoke to his brothers who had sold him into slavery: *"'You intended to harm me, but God intended it for good to accomplish what is now being done, the saving of many lives. So then, don't be afraid. I will provide for you and your children.' And he reassured them and spoke kindly to them."*

Joseph's ability to view the events of his life as coming through the filter of God's loving hands is exactly where we need to be. Certainly, Joseph did experience many losses, but his focus did not remain on those losses. He made the decision to rest in the fact God was in control of everything that had happened to him, and God was working it all for the good.

🏃 ACTION

Spend some time thinking about the story of Joseph. Try to imagine all he had endured and what he must have felt during different phases of his life. Next, draw a picture illustrating how you view God may be working in your challenging relationship(s) in the space provided. Of course, we do not always know how God is working. If you do not have any idea of what he may be doing, draw something illustrating God's sovereign hand even though you do not know exactly what he is doing. For example, you could draw a beautiful tapestry being woven from heaven, but all you can see from earth are the dangling, tangling threads. Or you could draw a picture of yourself resting in God's protection. Draw anything that will help you remember God is working out everything in your life for the good.

✏ JOURNAL

_____

_____

_____

_____

_____

_____

Friday

- Thank God for the help you received when you confessed your sin and received prayer from a friend.
- Recall the verse you memorized and check yourself to see if you are relying on your strength or God's in this relationship.
- If you need to address the repeated sin of the person with whom you are in a challenging relationship, be sure to follow the steps outlined in Matthew 18:15–20.
- Reflect on how your view of Scripture impacts your day-to-day life and the importance of lining up your beliefs with Scripture.
- Remember God is working everything out for the good in your life.
- Are you praying daily for your relationship?

✏️ **JOURNAL**

_____

_____

_____

_____

_____

_____

Week 9

Monday

📖 *Jeroboam thought to himself, "The kingdom will now likely revert to the house of David. If these people go up to offer sacrifices at the temple of the Lord in Jerusalem, they will again give their allegiance to their lord, Rehoboam king of Judah. They will kill me and return to King Rehoboam." (1 Kgs 12:26)*

WHEN DEALING WITH THE person with whom you are in a challenging relationship, are you ever tempted to "fix" things in a sinful way? In other words, after trying everything in your power in a good way to make things better, do you ever slip into sinful thoughts or actions? For example, sometimes people give into sexual temptation in an effort to make their dating relationships progress toward marriage. They may rationalize their decisions by thinking if they satisfy their boy/girlfriends sexually, they will be happier with them and will then decide to marry them. On the other hand, sometimes married men or women withhold their bodies from their spouses if they do not do what they want. Another example of when sinful behavior is used to try to bring about change in another person is when parents punish their children out of anger to make them obey. Obviously, this is not the way God wants parents to discipline their children, yet it is often done in an attempt to bring about positive results. In the story of King

Jeroboam from today's Scripture, we learn how he took matters into his own hands in a sinful way and ended up paying dearly for his decision. Let's take a closer look at this story.

In 1 Kings 11:37–38, we see where God presented an incredible gift to Jeroboam: he made him king! The Bible tells us God said:

> ". . . *I will take you, and you will rule over all that your heart desires; you will be king over Israel. If you do whatever I command you and walk in obedience to me and do what is right in my eyes by obeying my decrees and commands, as David my servant did, I will be with you. I will build you a dynasty as enduring as the one I built for David and will give Israel to you.*"

I don't know about you, but when I think about God giving a kingship to Jeroboam, it makes excited to see God's power in action and to see the awesome gifts he gives to people! I would hope Jeroboam was so thrilled by this opportunity he would have honored God's commands out of a thankful heart. Unfortunately, that was not the case.

In today's verses, we learn Jeroboam became concerned that if the Israelites had to go to the temple in Jerusalem to offer their required sacrifices, they would turn their allegiance back to their prior king Rehoboam and away from him. Instead of relying on God's promise to build him an enduring kingdom, Jeroboam allowed fear to rule over his decision-making process and created idols for the Israelites to worship. As a result, God tore the kingdom from Jeroboam's rule, and a series of other disastrous events came upon him. After Jeroboam made two golden calves for the people to worship, this is what God said to him:

> "*Go, tell Jeroboam that this is what the LORD, the God of Israel, says: 'I raised you up from among the people and appointed you ruler over my people Israel. I tore the kingdom away from the house of David and gave it to you, but you have not been like my servant David, who kept my commands and followed me with all his heart, doing only what was right in my eyes. You have done more evil than all who lived before you. You have made for yourself other*

gods, idols made of metal; you have aroused my anger and turned your back on me. Because of this, I am going to bring disaster on the house of Jeroboam. I will cut off from Jeroboam every last male in Israel—slave or free. I will burn up the house of Jeroboam as one burns dung, until it is all gone. Dogs will eat those belonging to Jeroboam who die in the city, and the birds will feed on those who die in the country. The LORD has spoken!" (1 Kgs 14:7–11).

This story and others like it where we vividly see God's discipline displayed send chills down my spine. This type of story is repeatedly told in the Bible, yet we tend to focus only on the kind and merciful side of God, while forgetting about the disciplinary side. You may think this type of situation was only in the Old Testament before Jesus came, but that is not the case. Even in the New Testament we find illustrations of God's anger toward sin and rebellion (see, for example, the story of Jesus displaying his anger in the temple in John 2:14–16, and the story about the deaths of Ananias and Sapphira due to their sin in Acts 5:1–11).

Is God loving and merciful? Yes. Does God discipline his children for their sin? Yes. In fact, God's discipline of his children is an indication of his love: *"And have you completely forgotten this word of encouragement that addresses you as a father addresses his son? It says, 'My son, do not make light of the Lord's discipline, and do not lose heart when he rebukes you, because the Lord disciplines the one he loves, and he chastens everyone he accepts as his son'"* (Heb 12:5–6). God is loving and merciful *and* he expects his children to be obedient to him.

✗ ACTION

Are there any sinful actions or thoughts you have committed or are currently committing in your relationship? If there are, confess them to God and remember: *"If we confess our sins, he is faithful and just and will forgive us our sins and purify us from all unrighteousness"* (1 John 1:9). Turn away from those practices and turn instead to trusting God and acting in accordance with his instructions for how we are to treat others.

✎ JOURNAL

_____

_____

_____

_____

_____

_____

Wednesday

Moses said to the LORD, "Pardon your servant, Lord. I have never been eloquent, neither in the past nor since you have spoken to your servant. I am slow of speech and tongue." The LORD said to him, "Who gave human beings their mouths? Who makes them deaf or mute? Who gives them sight or makes them blind? Is it not I, the LORD? Now go; I will help you speak and will teach you what to say." (Exod 4:10–12)

"... Not by might nor by power, but by my Spirit," says the LORD Almighty. (Zech 4:6)

DO YOU EVER FEEL completely inadequate in your relationship? Do you ever think you are not good enough to have this relationship? When times are tough between the two of you, do you consider all your personal shortcomings and think if you just possessed certain attributes or abilities (e.g., better temperament, better looking, more intelligent, thinner, taller, wealthier) things would improve? If you do, where do those thoughts lead? What actions do you take to try to correct those perceived shortcomings?

My guess is you might head to the gym if you think your weight is an issue. Perhaps if you think you are not smart enough, you might try to increase your knowledge by reading more. If you do not think you are attractive enough, maybe you spend more time fixing your hair or you may buy more clothes to enhance your appearance. On the other hand, you might begin to turn inward and feel ashamed or embarrassed about who you are. But let me ask you, have any of those actions helped or healed your relationship?

Of course, it is not wrong to try to better yourself, but if your focus becomes solely on what you lack as the reason for the failures between the two of you, you are not trusting in the One who gave you this relationship in the first place. It may seem like such a simple solution to simply trust God and turn everything over to him, but that is what the Bible teaches us about all matters in life.

In the verses prior to those given in Exodus above, the Lord had just commanded Moses to go tell the king of Egypt to give the Israelites their freedom. To say this was a huge assignment is putting it mildly! There were over a million Israelites who were slaves in Egypt doing all the heavy labor there. If the Israelites were to leave, Pharaoh knew his building projects would come to a fast halt, and Moses knew he would not willingly submit to this request from anyone, let alone from him. After all, at that time Moses was a man without any recognized position in Egypt, therefore, he did not have any power or influence with the king.

In today's verses, we see Moses's response to God's command, which was to focus on his own attributes. Notice how God answers Moses's objections: he tells Moses it is not about him or anything he possesses. God tells Moses he will empower him ("*I will help you speak*") and guide him ("*I will teach you what to say*"). You probably know the rest of the story. Through Moses and Aaron, God freed the Israelites from their captivity in Egypt by performing incredible miracles: blood in the Nile River, frogs, turning the dust of the land into gnats, swarms of flies, death of all the Egyptians' livestock, festering boils on the people and animals, hail, locusts, total darkness for three days, death to the firstborn of all the Egyptians, and the parting of the Red Sea.

You may be wondering how the ten plagues in Egypt and the story of Moses applies to you and your relationship. It comes down to a question of belief. Do you believe God was powerful enough to bring about the ten plagues? Do you believe he parted the Red Sea? If you answered yes, do you believe God is powerful enough to give you everything you need? If you say, "Yes, God is powerful enough to give me everything I need," but then you take matters into your own hands to try to help things along, are you acting in accordance with your beliefs? Are you relying on your beauty, strength, charm, hard work, intelligence, money, etc., to repair the brokenness between you instead of trusting God to do the work?

ACTION

Today's Action assignment is for you to rest in God's power. That's it. Simply hand the relationship back to God (I know, for probably the millionth time) and rest in his might and his power. I do not mean you should stop doing the things you know are the right things to do in your relationship. What I am suggesting is you set aside any actions arising from your desire to control or shape your relationship by some power or talent you possess.

JOURNAL

Friday

📖 *In the desert the whole community grumbled against Moses and Aaron. The Israelites said to them, "If only we had died by the LORD's hand in Egypt! There we sat around pots of meat and ate all the food we wanted, but you have brought us out into this desert to starve this entire assembly to death." (Exod 16:2–3)*

All the Israelites grumbled against Moses and Aaron, and the whole assembly said to them, "If only we had died in Egypt! Or in this wilderness! Why is the LORD bringing us to this land only to let us fall by the sword? Our wives and children will be taken as plunder. Wouldn't it be better for us to go back to Egypt?" (Num 14:2–3)

IT MAY SEEM INCREDIBLE that after witnessing the ten plagues and the parting of the Red Sea the Israelites would wish they could go back to the land of their enslavement in Egypt, but that is exactly what we see in these verses. In the verses in Exodus, the Israelites had been in the desert two and a half months following their departure from Egypt (Exod 16:1). They declared their displeasure with the situation by grumbling against Moses and Aaron, telling them they were better off in captivity. In the verses in Numbers, the Israelites are again complaining, but this time it was because they had just been told the Promised Land had obstacles they would need to overcome after they took possession of it. In both cases, the Israelites failed to remember how the Lord had worked miraculously on their behalf to help them escape their enslavement. As spectacular as those miracles were, they had lost sight of them and were focusing on their current situations.

Sometimes when we are struggling in a relationship, we can become so wrapped up in its problems we lose sight of God's mighty works. As a result, our problem-focused orientation leads us to believe we would be better off without the other person in our life at all. Chances are, however, the relationship you are working on is not one where the option to exit is a good one. A glance back through time at God's mighty works in your life can often result in a more hopeful perspective for the future.

ACTION

Spend time reflecting on your life since you have been in this relationship. Remember some specific situations in this relationship in which the Lord united, rescued, delivered, sustained, or healed you and write about them below. Then spend time thanking God for his mighty work on your behalf in the past and affirm your belief in his ability and his willingness to work again now.

_____

_____

_____

_____

_____

_____

✎ JOURNAL

_____

_____

_____

_____

_____

_____

Monday

📖 *Love the LORD your God with all your heart and with all your soul and with all your strength. (Deut 6:5)*

But be very careful to keep the commandment and the law that Moses the servant of the LORD gave you: to love the LORD your God, to walk in obedience to him, to keep his commands, to hold fast to him and to serve him with all your heart and with all your soul." (Josh 22:5)

"Teacher, which is the greatest commandment in the Law?" Jesus replied: "'Love the Lord your God with all your heart and with all your soul and with all your mind.' This is the first and greatest commandment." (Matt 22:36–38)

SOMETIMES THERE ARE RIVALRIES occurring in our hearts. A rivalry of the heart is when there is a competition for our love. In the case of keeping the greatest commandment to love the Lord with all our heart, soul, and mind, we must keep a check on who is getting first priority in our lives: God, something, or someone else.

I am sure you have witnessed relationships where a natural and good love have gone awry due to an almost obsessive devotion to a person. For example, a mother's love for a child, which is beautiful and necessary, can become distorted when it receives top billing above the love for God in her heart. In the case of spousal love, which is good and a gift from God, that, too, can become unhealthy and unbalanced if the love rivals the love for God. In these situations, as in all human relationships, it is essential to love God above all else.

You may be wondering how exactly we are to do that since God is not visible like our human loves. First, we must be committed to making him a priority in our lives, just as we would choose to do for a human relationship we are interested in developing. In a practical sense, that means spending time talking with him daily. It also means reading his word because you cannot know who God is without knowing what the Bible says about him: *"In the beginning was the Word, and the Word was with God, and the Word was God"* (John 1:1). If you say you love God but do not take time to read his letters to you, what does that indicate about your love for him? Think about it this way. If your spouse was to write you a letter and pour out his or her heart to you, and you let it sit around for years without ever opening it, what would that say to your spouse? In the same way, if we neglect the written word of God, what do our actions (or lack thereof) demonstrate about our love for him? Lastly, loving God with all your heart, soul, and strength means being obedient to what he has written in his word: *"If you love me, keep my commands"* (John 14:15).

⚡ ACTION

Below are a series of questions to help you begin to assess whether you are loving the Lord with all your heart, soul, and mind. Ask yourself these questions and then write the answers below. Be specific and detailed in your responses.

Do I set aside time every day to pray?

_____

_____

_____

If the answer was no: What would be the best time of day for me to set aside every day to pray?

_____

_____

_____

Do I need to let others know I am making this commitment so they will not interrupt that time and/or so they can encourage me to establish this pattern?

_____

_____

_____

When will I start this?

_____

_____

_____

Do I read the Bible daily?

_____

_____

_____

If not, how can I make time to do this?

_____

_____

_____

Do I need to get others involved to help me stay committed to this as I did with the prayer time?

_____

_____

_____

Do I know how to start reading the Bible?

_____

_____

_____

If not, who can I talk to who can help me know where to begin?

_____

_____

_____

When will I call that person for help?

_____

_____

_____

When will I start reading my Bible daily?

_____

_____

_____

Are there any sins I am committing?

_____

_____

_____

Am I willing to give them up?

_____

_____

_____

Have I confessed them to God?

_____

_____

_____

If not, am I willing to do that now?

_____

_____

_____

When will I give them up?

_____

_____

_____

Do I need help in stopping them?

_____

_____

_____

If yes, who will I call or go see for help (e.g., a friend, relative, pastor, counselor, support group)?

_____

_____

_____

If I intend to seek help, when will I call or see the person or group named above?

_____

_____

_____

✐ JOURNAL

_____

_____

_____

_____

_____

_____

Wednesday

A song. A psalm of David. My heart, O God, is steadfast; I will sing and make music with all my soul. Awake, harp and lyre! I will awaken the dawn. I will praise you, LORD, among the nations; I will sing of you among the peoples. For great is your love, higher than the heavens; your faithfulness reaches to the skies. Be exalted, O God, above the heavens; let your glory be over all the earth. (Ps 108:1–5)

Do not get drunk on wine which leads to debauchery. Instead, be filled with the Spirit, speaking to one another with psalms, hymns, and songs from the Spirit. Sing and make music from your heart to the Lord, always giving thanks to God the Father for everything, in the Name of our Lord Jesus Christ. (Eph 5:18–20)

WE CANNOT BE RIGHT with the people in our lives unless we are right with God. That is why today (like other days we have covered previously) the focus is on your relationship with the Lord.

Since we are in a relationship with the creator of the universe, there is much for which we can be grateful. In today's verses, we see how David thought about some of the blessings he received from God such as his love and his faithfulness, and that caused him to rejoice and sing to him. Praising God in song is one way of showing our love and appreciation to him.

𝑅 ACTION

Are you in the habit of singing to God outside of church? Think about some benefits you have received from the Lord and sing to him about them. If you do not think you have a great singing voice, don't worry about it! God made your voice and loves it no matter how you think it sounds. Let the words flow from your heart with joy as an offering to him.

✎ JOURNAL

_____

_____

_____

_____

_____

_____

Friday

↰ REVIEW

- Are you allowing sin to remain in your relationship?
- Reflect on any internal or external qualities you possess that you need to set aside so God's strength and power can reign in your relationship.
- Remember some of the ways the Lord has worked in your life in the past.
- Have you started making changes that will help you love the Lord with all your heart, soul, and mind?
- Sing to the Lord.
- Are you praying daily for your relationship?

JOURNAL

_____

_____

_____

_____

_____

_____

Conclusion

YOU HAVE SPENT THE past ten weeks reading this book, working on the assignments, and journaling what you have learned and experienced. You read Scripture and completed Action assignments directly involving the person with whom you have a challenging relationship. Additionally, you read Scripture and completed assignments focused on your relationship with the Lord. While the purpose of this study was to help you with one or more challenging relationships in your life, it is my strong conviction that in order to manage those well you must also maintain a healthy relationship with God. If your vertical relationship (with God) is unhealthy, your horizontal relationships (with people) will be negatively impacted. In other words, the time and energy you devote to your relationship with the Lord will overflow into your human relationships.

That being the case, as you spend time evaluating the impact of this study, my hope is you will notice a positive change in the quality of your relationship with Jesus. I hope you will see his impressions on your thoughts and actions more vividly than when you began, and you will love him and his Word more as a result. In addition, I hope you will understand more fully how the Lord wants you to handle your relationships, the easy as well as the difficult ones. It is also my desire that you are more likely now than before you began this study to sift your actions and reactions through the filter of the Bible.

Since challenging relationships are generally the product of years of complex interactions, they are not likely to resolve and become healthy after a few weeks of study and action assignments. As I wrote in the beginning of this book, I believe once you complete this study you might want to go back and do it again to make the principles from Scripture sink in more deeply. Furthermore, by going through the book and doing the Action assignments again, you will have a greater opportunity to make the new ways of acting take hold in your life.

At the beginning of the book and throughout it, I encouraged you to pray daily about your relationship(s) because the source of all your strength and power is from God. As you continue to love well when times are good and when they are difficult, remember to rest in the fact that God is sovereign over (i.e., in control of) everything, including your relationships:

> Yours, LORD, is the greatness and the power and the glory and the majesty and the splendor, for everything in heaven and earth is yours. Yours, LORD, is the kingdom; you are exalted as head over all. Wealth and honor come from you; you are the ruler of all things. In your hands are strength and power to exalt and give strength to all. Now, our God, we give you thanks, and praise your glorious Name (1 Chr 29:11–13).

The Plan of Salvation

SALVATION MEANS YOU BELIEVE Jesus Christ obtained eternal life in heaven for you when he died on the cross for your sins. It means you believe that Jesus, who is God's Son, came to earth as a human, lived a perfect life, then was crucified to pay the penalty for your sins: "*For God so loved the world that he gave his one and only Son, that whoever believes in him shall not perish but have eternal life*" (John 3:16); "*If you declare with your mouth, 'Jesus is Lord,' and believe in your heart that God raised him from the dead, you will be saved. For it is with your heart that you believe and are justified, and it is with your mouth that you profess your faith and are saved*" (Rom 10:9–10); "*For it is by grace you have been saved, through faith—and this is not from yourselves, it is the gift of God—not by works, so that no one can boast*" (Eph 2:8–9).

Salvation is a gift from God. You do not earn it, nor do you do anything to deserve it: "*For the wages of sin is death, but the gift of God is eternal life in Christ Jesus our Lord*" (Rom 6:23). If you desire to know God and want to have a personal relationship with him, it is because God himself is stirring in your heart that desire.

When you receive salvation from Christ, acknowledge that Jesus is your Lord which means you will live your life in obedience to him: "*Then he called the crowd to him along with his disciples and said: 'Whoever wants to be my disciple must deny themselves and take up their cross and follow me. For whoever wants to save their life will lose it, but whoever loses their life for me and for the Gospel will save it. What good is it for someone to gain the whole world, yet forfeit their soul?'"* (Mark 8:34–36). Turn away from your sins (this is called repentance) and pursue living for God: *"Repent and be baptized, every one of you, in the Name of Jesus Christ for the forgiveness of your sins. And you will receive the gift of the Holy Spirit"* (Acts 2:38).

You will also want to contact a biblically sound church and tell the pastor you have accepted Christ as your Savior so he can help you begin your new life. If you are not sure how to find a Bible-based church, email me at weyer.nancy@gmail.com and I will be happy to welcome you into the family of believers and help you get started.

Remember, if you are reading this plan of salvation and feel drawn to God, it is because he is drawing you, so do not take that lightly: *"For he says, 'In the time of my favor I heard you, and in the day of salvation I helped you.' I tell you, now is the time of God's favor, now is the day of salvation"* (2 Cor 6:2).

True

Honorable

Right

Pure

Lovely

Excellent

Admirable

Worthy of Praise

Bibliography

Blue Letter Bible. "Lexicon: Strong's G25—*agapaō*." https://www.blueletterbible.
org/lexicon/g25/niv/mgnt/0-1/.

Kenneth L. Barker, ed. *NIV Study Bible: New International Version.* Grand
Rapids, MI: Zondervan, 1985.

Merriam-Webster's Collegiate Dictionary. 11th ed. Springfield, MA: Merriam-
Webster, 2003. Continually updated at https://www.merriam-webster.
com/.

www.ingramcontent.com/pod-product-compliance
Lightning Source LLC
Chambersburg PA
CBHW071050090426
42737CB00013B/2308